Greetings and salutations! Thank you for purchasing my dream journal. I pray this book will inspire you to write down your dreams and wait and listen to hear what God says when He speaks to you. May the heavens open while you sleep.

-Apostle Delmarva Johnson

GW00467703

Acknowledgements

To my mother, Helen Johnson, who continues to encourage me, push me, and believe in me

To Daron Baldwin, for seeing my vision for this book cover and executing it with perfection and timeliness

To Dionne and Imani Johnson, this book would not be, if it had not been for your devoted editing. Thank you for loving me!

Testimonials

"Apostle Delmarva's book has a wealth of knowledge concerning the spiritual realm. By the revelation of the Holy Spirit, she has taught many about prophetic dreams and visions. This book has inspired me to dig deeper into the Word of God to increase my seeking for the mysteries of the Spirit and gain more wisdom, knowledge, and understanding. If you would like to be enlightened to a deeper place in dreams and visions in the prophetic arena, then this is definitely a "must read"!"

Minister Naveesa Nixon
Warriors of Christ Church, Atlanta, GA
Student of the School of the Prophets - Fresh Oil

"One important aspect of dreams you will learn is to always rely on the Holy Spirits interpretation of the dream. How to always seek the Father first. Scripture is the first and final authority even with the foundational meaning of certain things. Things book will also show you how even those symbols mean something completely different based off of the context of the dream. Apostle Johnson reaffirms that context is key to understanding your dreams. You will learn the difference between dreams from God, soulish dreams and dreams from the enemy. Another important aspect you will learn is that time belongs to God. He will give you the interpretation at the right time. A must-read book of impartation that will unlock deep dimensions of your dream life and will activate a deeper seeker in you."

Prophet Tanty Freeman ll
Community Prayer House
Student of The School of Prophets - Fresh Oil

"Apostle Johnson is an incredible woman of God. I have been taking her spiritual warfare and dream classes for 2 years now and have grown so much in wisdom. I love hearing her warfare experiences and am at awe when I see her warfare in practice! I have applied her teachings to my everyday life and have seen the hand of God move. I am overly excited about her new dream book! Her pastorship lead me to a realm of God, I never knew exist."

Nikki Campbell, Celebrity Makeup Artist, BluArtistry
Warriors of Christ Church, Tennessee
Student of the School of the Prophets - Fresh Oil

Copyright © 2019 by Delmarva Johnson

All rights reserved. No part of this book may be reproduced in any form or by any electronic or mechanical means, including information storage and retrieval systems, without permission in writing from the publisher, except by reviewers, who may quote brief passages in a review.

All photos/images were paid for and used through the Over App

Scripture quotations marked KJV are taken from the King James Version. Public Domain.

Scripture taken from the New King James Version. Copyright © by Thomas Nelson, Inc. Used by Permission. All rights reserved.

Cover Design by Daron Baldwin, Mister Creative Designs

Printed in the United States of America

Published by Kindle Direct Publishing

Table of Contents

Entering into the Dream World Journal 1

Colors.. 6

Numbers.. 7

Levels.. 9

Prayer Watches.. 11

Journal Pages... 18

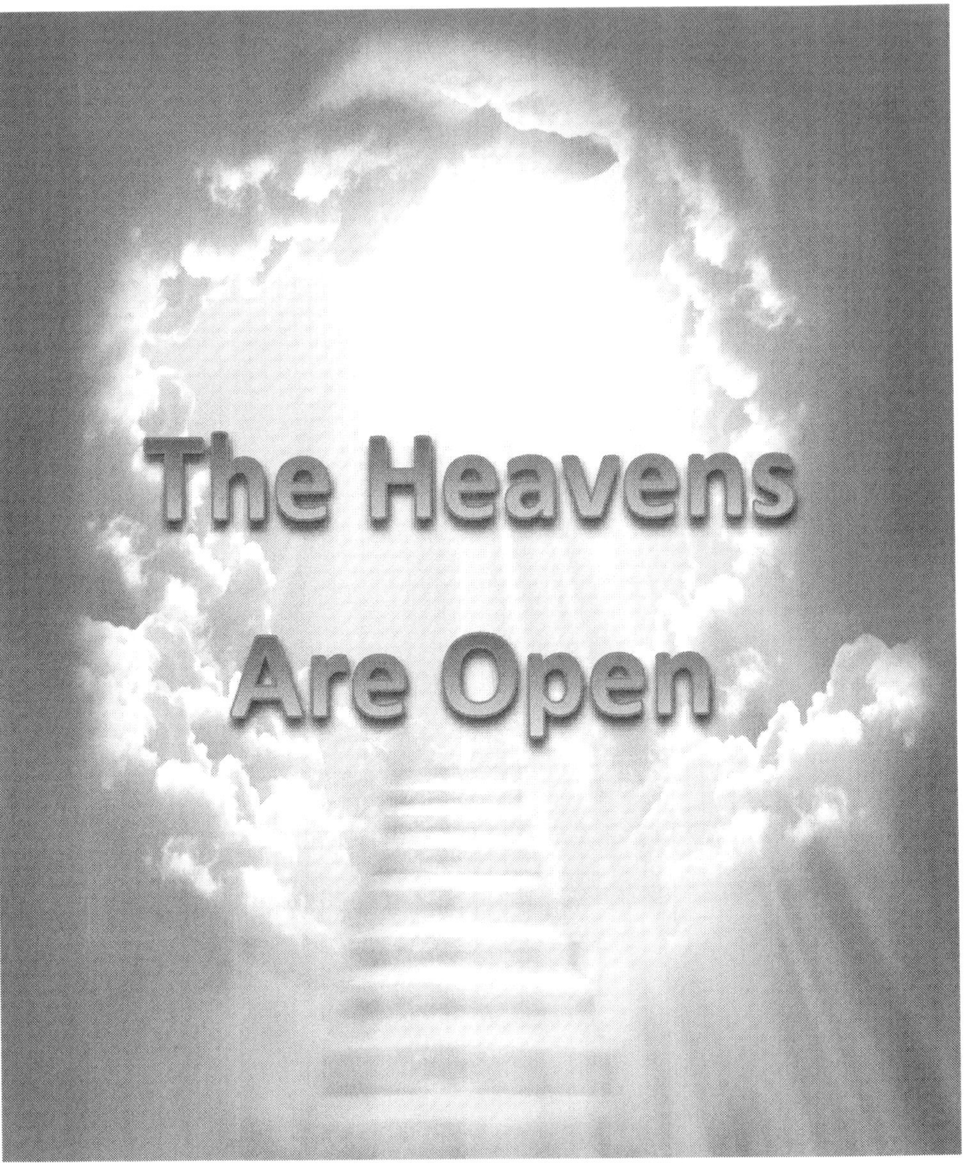
The Heavens
Are Open

Entering into the Dream World Journal

Dreams are ways God communicates with us. There is so much He wants to share with us. He loves to play hide and seek when communicating with His creation. Look what the Word has to say about seeking Him:

Proverbs 8:17 King James Version (KJV) - "I love those who love me, and those who seek me."

Jeremiah 29:13 (KJV) - "You will seek me and find me when you seek me with your WHOLE heart."

He has one requirement, that if we seek Him, we must do it with our whole heart. If we do that, then we will find him. How exciting is that? Knowing you can find God in hidden places!

There are times when God will hide himself from us.

Isaiah 45:15 - "Truly you are the God who hides himself, O God of Israel, Savior!"

Isaiah 8:17 - "And I will wait for the Lord who is hiding his face from the house of Jacob; I will even look eagerly for him."

When He speaks through dreams, sometimes we don't understand what He is saying, so He makes us seek him for the answer. Some dreams are crazy. You wake up like, "What???" But the whole time there was a message in the dream. He uses colors, objects, numbers, places, things and people; however, this dream journal will only talk about colors and numbers.

In our dream life, we have heavenly encounters, so I encourage you to keep this journal and a pen and wait to see what He says.

Make sure you write down the things that stick out to you the most. When seeking God concerning the message, you must find the source. There are three different sources for our dreams:
1. God
2. The Soulish Realm
3. The Demonic Realm

Always remember this scripture: Ecclesiastes 5:3a, "For a dream comes through much activity."

There are often times that we dream by things we encounter during the day, or what's weighing on our hearts.

Not every dream is from God and not every dream is significant. Some dreams can simply be wishful thinking.

In the Bible, you will see that God communicated with both Godly and ungodly men through dreams. In the ancient Near East, dreams were one of several ways people sought to see their future and to make decisions that would benefit them.

Some societies went to temples or holy places to sleep in order to have a dream to show them what decisions they needed to make.

It's very important to not only seek God concerning every dream, but to wait on his response, which could take hours, days or weeks.

In Genesis, Joseph tells us that interpretation belongs to God. Genesis 40:8 (KJV) says this: "And they said unto him, We have dreamed a dream, and there is no interpreter of it. And

Joseph said unto them, Do not interpretations belong to God? Tell me them, I pray you."

Jeremiah and Zechariah did not solely rely on dreams without getting revelation from God. The following scriptures give us an insight on how we should go to God concerning our dreams and the source from which they've come.

Jeremiah 23:28 (KJV) says, "The prophet that hath a dream, let him tell a dream; and he that hath my word, let him speak my word faithfully. What is the chaff to the wheat? saith the Lord."

Jeremiah 29:8 (KJV) says, "For thus saith the Lord of hosts, the God of Israel; Let not your prophets and your diviners, that be in the midst of you, deceive you, neither hearken to your dreams which ye cause to be dreamed."

Zechariah 10:1-2 (KJV)
1 Ask ye of the Lord rain in the time of the latter rain; so the Lord shall make bright clouds, and give them showers of rain, to every one grass in the field.

2 For the idols have spoken vanity, and the diviners have seen a lie, and have told false dreams; they comfort in vain: therefore they went their way as a flock, they were troubled, because there was no shepherd.

When people tell you they have a dream concerning you, consider the source and ask the Holy Spirit for revelation to know if it came from God.

When interpreting, pay attention to what you see, such as people, places, colors, objects, animals and numbers.

COLORS

Red - fire, covers our sins and protection
Joshua 2:18, Exodus 12:7 and Matthew 26:28

Yellow - glory
Psalms 68:13

Green - healing and prosperity
1 King 10:27, Psalms 92:12
Cedar represents wealth

Purple - royalty, royal birth, kingship and majesty
Songs of Solomon 7:5, Luke 16:19

Blue - heaven, authority and revelation
Exodus 24:10, Esther 1:15

Black - death and mourning
Job 30:28, Jeremiah 14:2

White - holy, purity and angels
Acts 1:10, Revelation 4:4

1 - singleness, unity
Deuteronomy 6:4

2 - witness, new life, financial increase/
multiplication
Adam and Eve created life together it took both
of them
Genesis 1:28

3 - completion, perfection
Jesus was resurrected on the third day
Matthew 12:40, 1 Peter 3:19

4 - the world, creation
The earth has four directions (east, west, north
and south)
The earth has four seasons (spring, summer,
fall and winter)
Revelation 7:1

5 - grace, miracle to multiply
Joseph's Grace
Jesus gave the church the fivefold ministry (We
need grace to walk in these offices)
Genesis 43:34, Ephesians 4:11-13

6 - human weakness, fall, satan
Genesis 1:31

7 - Perfection
God rested
Genesis 2:2, Matthew 18:22

8 - New Beginning
John 20:26

9 - The number of the Holy Spirit, New birth
1 Corinthians 12:1-11

10 - Divine Government, Authority
God gave Moses the Ten Commandments,
establishing order for the Israelites
Deuteronomy 4:13

There are three different levels to our dreams. Some will achieve the third level without any effort, but others will find it only comes with activation and maturity in the things of God.

Level 1

When God is speaking to you and you're not clear what he is saying. This is the level where you can't interpret your own dreams and need an interpreter.

Job 33:14-15 (KJV)
14 For God speaketh once, yea twice, yet man perceiveth it not.

15 In a dream, in a vision of the night, when deep sleep falleth upon men, in slumberings upon the bed;

Level 2

In this realm you may understand pieces of your dreams. Everything is symbolic and you have to meditate and pray for understanding.

Level 3

In this realm, you will see the dream come to pass exactly as you saw it.

Prayer watches will help you to discern which watch you are on. Pay attention to what time you wake up from your dream. When journaling, write down the time and the date. Below, I have listed the prayer watches and their respective times:

The First Watch (6:00pm - 9:00pm)

This watch is known for physical, spiritual, and mental healing.

Matthew 14:14-15 New King James Version (NKJV)
14 And when Jesus went out, He saw a great multitude; and He was moved with compassion for them, and healed their sick.

15 When it was evening, His disciples came to Him, saying, "This is a deserted place, and the hour is already late. Send the multitudes away, that they may go into the villages and buy themselves food."

Mark 1:2 (NKJV)

2 As it is written in the Prophets: "Behold, I send My messenger before Your face, Who will prepare Your way before You."

This watch is also the time for the gatekeepers to possess the gates of the enemy to break curses.

The Second Watch (9:00pm - Midnight)

This watch is of the breakers' anointing. In this watch, pray that God breaks the chains off those who are bound. He will fight against those who are fighting against you and release protection for you.

Acts 16:25 (KJV)

25 And at midnight Paul and Silas prayed, and sang praises unto God: and the prisoners heard them.

Exodus 3:19-20 (KJV)

19 And I am sure that the king of Egypt will not let you go, no, not by a mighty hand.

20 And I will stretch out my hand and smite Egypt with all my wonders which I will do in the midst thereof: and after that he will let you go.

Exodus 12:29 (KJV)
29 And it came to pass, that at midnight the Lord smote all the firstborn in the land of Egypt, from the firstborn of Pharaoh that sat on his throne unto the firstborn of the captive that was in the dungeon; and all the firstborn of cattle.

Psalm 35:1 (KJV)
1 Plead my cause, O Lord, with them that strive with me: fight against them that fight against me.

Zechariah 1:10-11 (KJV)
10 And the man that stood among the myrtle trees answered and said, These are they whom the Lord hath sent to walk to and fro through the earth.

11 And they answered the angel of the Lord that stood among the myrtle trees, and said, We have walked to and fro through the earth, and, behold, all the earth sitteth still, and is at rest.

The Third Watch (12:00am - 3:00 am)

I like to call this watch "The Satanic Hours". Nine times out of ten, these are the hours you will be awakened by demonic presences or by a nightmare. These are the hours the devil likes to torment people. During these hours, he'll hold satanic meetings concerning you and your family, then he'll send demons out on assignment to try and attack you.

I have personally, on several occasions, experienced demons visiting me during these hours. I overcame them by the BLOOD of the Lamb. Whenever an attack like this happens, begin to plead the blood of Jesus and call on the name of Jesus and the attack will stop.

Here are some scriptures in which we learn about activity during this watch:

In 1 Kings 3:20 (KJV), we see how a woman plotted and stole another woman's child at midnight. "And she arose at midnight, and took my son from beside me, while thine handmaid slept, and laid it in her bosom, and laid her dead child in my bosom."

Matthew 13:25 (KJV) says, "But while men slept, his enemy came and sowed tares among the wheat, and went his way."

The Fourth Watch (3:00 am - 6:00 am)

I like to call this watch "When Heaven Touches Earth." You will experience supernatural activities during these hours. We can see heaven touch earth during these hours in the 14th chapter of Matthew:

Matthew 14:25-26 (KJV):
25 And in the fourth watch of the night Jesus went unto them, walking on the sea.

26 And when the disciples saw him walking on the sea, they were troubled, saying, It is a spirit; and they cried out for fear.

Genesis 32:24 shows us supernatural activity when Jacob wrestles with the Angel:
24 And Jacob was left alone; and there wrestled a man with him until the breaking of the day.

25 And when he saw that he prevailed not against him, he touched the hollow of his thigh; and the hollow of Jacob's thigh was out of joint, as he wrestled with him.

26 And he said, Let me go, for the day breaketh. And he said, I will not let thee go, except thou bless me.

27 And he said unto him, What is thy name? And he said, Jacob.

28 And he said, Thy name shall be called no more Jacob, but Israel: for as a prince hast thou power with God and with men, and hast prevailed.

29 And Jacob asked him, and said, Tell me, I pray thee, thy name. And he said, Wherefore is it that thou dost ask after my name? And he blessed him there.

The
Dream
Journal

God sends message & instructions
through dreams
Matthew 2: 13-23 KJV

13 And when they were
departed, behold, the angel of the
Lord appeareth to Joseph in a
dream, saying, Arise, and take
the young child and his mother,
and flee into Egypt, and be thou
there until I bring thee word: for
Herod will seek the young child
to destroy him.

But the Comforter, which is the Holy Ghost, whom the Father will send in my name, he shall teach you all things, and bring all things to your remembrance, whatsoever I have said unto you. John 14:26 (KJV)

Date and Time of Dream: _____

_____

_____

_____

_____

_____

_____

_____

_____

_____

_____

_____

_____

_____

_____

_____

_____

_____

_____

_____

But the Comforter, which is the Holy Ghost, whom the Father will send in my name, he shall teach you all things, and bring all things to your remembrance, whatsoever I have said unto you. John 14:26 (KJV)

But the Comforter, which is the Holy Ghost, whom the Father will send in my name, he shall teach you all things, and bring all things to your remembrance, whatsoever I have said unto you. John 14:26 (KJV)

But the Comforter, which is the Holy Ghost, whom the Father will send in my name, he shall teach you all things, and bring all things to your remembrance, whatsoever I have said unto you. John 14:26 (KJV)

_____

_____

_____

_____

_____

_____

_____

_____

_____

_____

_____

_____

_____

_____

_____

_____

_____

_____

But the Comforter, which is the Holy Ghost, whom the Father will send in my name, he shall teach you all things, and bring all things to your remembrance, whatsoever I have said unto you. John 14:26 (KJV)

_____

_____

_____

_____

_____

_____

_____

_____

_____

_____

_____

_____

_____

_____

_____

_____

_____

_____

_____

Numbers 12: 6-8 KJV

And he said, Hear now my words: If there be a prophet among you, I the Lord will make myself known unto him in a vision, and will speak unto him in a dream.

But the Comforter, which is the Holy Ghost, whom the Father will send in my name, he shall teach you all things, and bring all things to your remembrance, whatsoever I have said unto you. John 14:26 (KJV)

Date and Time of Dream: _____

_____

_____

_____

_____

_____

_____

_____

_____

_____

_____

_____

_____

_____

_____

_____

_____

_____

_____

_____

_____

But the Comforter, which is the Holy Ghost, whom the Father will send in my name, he shall teach you all things, and bring all things to your remembrance, whatsoever I have said unto you. John 14:26 (KJV)

But the Comforter, which is the Holy Ghost, whom the Father will send in my name, he shall teach you all things, and bring all things to your remembrance, whatsoever I have said unto you. John 14:26 (KJV)

_____

_____

_____

_____

_____

_____

_____

_____

_____

_____

_____

_____

_____

_____

_____

_____

_____

_____

But the Comforter, which is the Holy Ghost, whom the Father will send in my name, he shall teach you all things, and bring all things to your remembrance, whatsoever I have said unto you. John 14:26 (KJV)

But the Comforter, which is the Holy Ghost, whom the Father will send in my name, he shall teach you all things, and bring all things to your remembrance, whatsoever I have said unto you. John 14:26 (KJV)

_____

_____

_____

_____

_____

_____

_____

_____

_____

_____

_____

_____

_____

_____

_____

_____

Set a goal that makes you want to jump out of bed

But the Comforter, which is the Holy Ghost, whom the Father will send in my name, he shall teach you all things, and bring all things to your remembrance, whatsoever I have said unto you. John 14:26 (KJV)

Date and Time of Dream: _____

_____

_____

_____

_____

_____

_____

_____

_____

_____

_____

_____

_____

_____

_____

_____

_____

_____

_____

But the Comforter, which is the Holy Ghost, whom the Father will send in my name, he shall teach you all things, and bring all things to your remembrance, whatsoever I have said unto you. John 14:26 (KJV)

But the Comforter, which is the Holy Ghost, whom the Father will send in my name, he shall teach you all things, and bring all things to your remembrance, whatsoever I have said unto you. John 14:26 (KJV)

But the Comforter, which is the Holy Ghost, whom the Father will send in my name, he shall teach you all things, and bring all things to your remembrance, whatsoever I have said unto you. John 14:26 (KJV)

_____

_____

_____

_____

_____

_____

_____

_____

_____

_____

_____

_____

_____

_____

_____

_____

_____

_____

_____

But the Comforter, which is the Holy Ghost, whom the Father will send in my name, he shall teach you all things, and bring all things to your remembrance, whatsoever I have said unto you. John 14:26 (KJV)

Psalm 118:24 King James Version (KJV)

This is the day which the Lord hath made; we will rejoice and be glad in it.

But the Comforter, which is the Holy Ghost, whom the Father will send in my name, he shall teach you all things, and bring all things to your remembrance, whatsoever I have said unto you. John 14:26 (KJV)

Date and Time of Dream: _____

_____

_____

_____

_____

_____

_____

_____

_____

_____

_____

_____

_____

_____

_____

_____

_____

_____

_____

_____

But the Comforter, which is the Holy Ghost, whom the Father will send in my name, he shall teach you all things, and bring all things to your remembrance, whatsoever I have said unto you. John 14:26 (KJV)

But the Comforter, which is the Holy Ghost, whom the Father will send in my name, he shall teach you all things, and bring all things to your remembrance, whatsoever I have said unto you. John 14:26 (KJV)

_____

_____

_____

_____

_____

_____

_____

_____

_____

_____

_____

_____

_____

_____

_____

_____

_____

But the Comforter, which is the Holy Ghost, whom the Father will send in my name, he shall teach you all things, and bring all things to your remembrance, whatsoever I have said unto you. John 14:26 (KJV)

But the Comforter, which is the Holy Ghost, whom the Father will send in my name, he shall teach you all things, and bring all things to your remembrance, whatsoever I have said unto you. John 14:26 (KJV)

_____

_____

_____

_____

_____

_____

_____

_____

_____

_____

_____

_____

_____

_____

_____

_____

Today is a new day and yesterday is behind you

But the Comforter, which is the Holy Ghost, whom the Father will send in my name, he shall teach you all things, and bring all things to your remembrance, whatsoever I have said unto you. John 14:26 (KJV)

Date and Time of Dream: _____

_____

_____

_____

_____

_____

_____

_____

_____

_____

_____

_____

_____

_____

_____

_____

_____

_____

_____

_____

But the Comforter, which is the Holy Ghost, whom the Father will send in my name, he shall teach you all things, and bring all things to your remembrance, whatsoever I have said unto you. John 14:26 (KJV)

But the Comforter, which is the Holy Ghost, whom the Father will send in my name, he shall teach you all things, and bring all things to your remembrance, whatsoever I have said unto you. John 14:26 (KJV)

But the Comforter, which is the Holy Ghost, whom the Father will send in my name, he shall teach you all things, and bring all things to your remembrance, whatsoever I have said unto you. John 14:26 (KJV)

But the Comforter, which is the Holy Ghost, whom the Father will send in my name, he shall teach you all things, and bring all things to your remembrance, whatsoever I have said unto you. John 14:26 (KJV)

You have the power, to command your, morning

Job 38:12-13 New King James Version (NKJV)

12 "Have you commanded the morning since your, days began,

And caused the dawn to know its place

But the Comforter, which is the Holy Ghost, whom the Father will send in my name, he shall teach you all things, and bring all things to your remembrance, whatsoever I have said unto you. John 14:26 (KJV)

Date and Time of Dream: _____

_____

_____

_____

_____

_____

_____

_____

_____

_____

_____

_____

_____

_____

_____

_____

_____

_____

_____

_____

_____

But the Comforter, which is the Holy Ghost, whom the Father will send in my name, he shall teach you all things, and bring all things to your remembrance, whatsoever I have said unto you. John 14:26 (KJV)

_____

_____

_____

_____

_____

_____

_____

_____

_____

_____

_____

_____

_____

_____

_____

_____

_____

_____

_____

But the Comforter, which is the Holy Ghost, whom the Father will send in my name, he shall teach you all things, and bring all things to your remembrance, whatsoever I have said unto you. John 14:26 (KJV)

But the Comforter, which is the Holy Ghost, whom the Father will send in my name, he shall teach you all things, and bring all things to your remembrance, whatsoever I have said unto you. John 14:26 (KJV)

But the Comforter, which is the Holy Ghost, whom the Father will send in my name, he shall teach you all things, and bring all things to your remembrance, whatsoever I have said unto you. John 14:26 (KJV)

Dreams
come true

I will rejoice when he speaks

to me

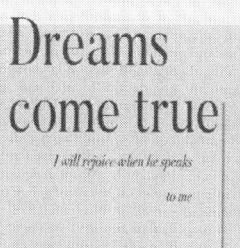

But the Comforter, which is the Holy Ghost, whom the Father will send in my name, he shall teach you all things, and bring all things to your remembrance, whatsoever I have said unto you. John 14:26 (KJV)

Date and Time of Dream: _____

_____

_____

_____

_____

_____

_____

_____

_____

_____

_____

_____

_____

_____

_____

_____

_____

_____

_____

_____

_____

But the Comforter, which is the Holy Ghost, whom the Father will send in my name, he shall teach you all things, and bring all things to your remembrance, whatsoever I have said unto you. John 14:26 (KJV)

But the Comforter, which is the Holy Ghost, whom the Father will send in my name, he shall teach you all things, and bring all things to your remembrance, whatsoever I have said unto you. John 14:26 (KJV)

But the Comforter, which is the Holy Ghost, whom the Father will send in my name, he shall teach you all things, and bring all things to your remembrance, whatsoever I have said unto you. John 14:26 (KJV)

But the Comforter, which is the Holy Ghost, whom the Father will send in my name, he shall teach you all things, and bring all things to your remembrance, whatsoever I have said unto you. John 14:26 (KJV)

I will both lay down in peace and sleep: for you, Lord, only makes the me dwell in safety

Psalms 4:8

But the Comforter, which is the Holy Ghost, whom the Father will send in my name, he shall teach you all things, and bring all things to your remembrance, whatsoever I have said unto you. John 14:26 (KJV)

Date and Time of Dream: _____

But the Comforter, which is the Holy Ghost, whom the Father will send in my name, he shall teach you all things, and bring all things to your remembrance, whatsoever I have said unto you. John 14:26 (KJV)

But the Comforter, which is the Holy Ghost, whom the Father will send in my name, he shall teach you all things, and bring all things to your remembrance, whatsoever I have said unto you. John 14:26 (KJV)

But the Comforter, which is the Holy Ghost, whom the Father will send in my name, he shall teach you all things, and bring all things to your remembrance, whatsoever I have said unto you. John 14:26 (KJV)

But the Comforter, which is the Holy Ghost, whom the Father will send in my name, he shall teach you all things, and bring all things to your remembrance, whatsoever I have said unto you. John 14:26 (KJV)

But thou, O Lord, art a shield for me: my glory, and the lifter up of mine head

Psalms 3:3-5

But the Comforter, which is the Holy Ghost, whom the Father will send in my name, he shall teach you all things, and bring all things to your remembrance, whatsoever I have said unto you. John 14:26 (KJV)

Date and Time of Dream: _____

_____

_____

_____

_____

_____

_____

_____

_____

_____

_____

_____

_____

_____

_____

_____

_____

_____

_____

_____

But the Comforter, which is the Holy Ghost, whom the Father will send in my name, he shall teach you all things, and bring all things to your remembrance, whatsoever I have said unto you. John 14:26 (KJV)

But the Comforter, which is the Holy Ghost, whom the Father will send in my name, he shall teach you all things, and bring all things to your remembrance, whatsoever I have said unto you. John 14:26 (KJV)

But the Comforter, which is the Holy Ghost, whom the Father will send in my name, he shall teach you all things, and bring all things to your remembrance, whatsoever I have said unto you. John 14:26 (KJV)

But the Comforter, which is the Holy Ghost, whom the Father will send in my name, he shall teach you all things, and bring all things to your remembrance, whatsoever I have said unto you. John 14:26 (KJV)

The Lord will watch over you while you sleep.
Psalms 121: 3-8

But the Comforter, which is the Holy Ghost, whom the Father will send in my name, he shall teach you all things, and bring all things to your remembrance, whatsoever I have said unto you. John 14:26 (KJV)

Date and Time of Dream: _____

_____

_____

_____

_____

_____

_____

_____

_____

_____

_____

_____

_____

_____

_____

_____

_____

_____

_____

_____

_____

But the Comforter, which is the Holy Ghost, whom the Father will send in my name, he shall teach you all things, and bring all things to your remembrance, whatsoever I have said unto you. John 14:26 (KJV)

But the Comforter, which is the Holy Ghost, whom the Father will send in my name, he shall teach you all things, and bring all things to your remembrance, whatsoever I have said unto you. John 14:26 (KJV)

But the Comforter, which is the Holy Ghost, whom the Father will send in my name, he shall teach you all things, and bring all things to your remembrance, whatsoever I have said unto you. John 14:26 (KJV)

But the Comforter, which is the Holy Ghost, whom the Father will send in my name, he shall teach you all things, and bring all things to your remembrance, whatsoever I have said unto you. John 14:26 (KJV)

Habakkuk 2:1 King James Version (KJV)

2 I will stand upon my watch, and set me upon the tower, and will watch to see what he will say unto me, and what I shall answer when I am reproved.

But the Comforter, which is the Holy Ghost, whom the Father will send in my name, he shall teach you all things, and bring all things to your remembrance, whatsoever I have said unto you. John 14:26 (KJV)

Date and Time of Dream: _____

_____

_____

_____

_____

_____

_____

_____

_____

_____

_____

_____

_____

_____

_____

_____

_____

_____

_____

_____

_____

But the Comforter, which is the Holy Ghost, whom the Father will send in my name, he shall teach you all things, and bring all things to your remembrance, whatsoever I have said unto you. John 14:26 (KJV)

But the Comforter, which is the Holy Ghost, whom the Father will send in my name, he shall teach you all things, and bring all things to your remembrance, whatsoever I have said unto you. John 14:26 (KJV)

But the Comforter, which is the Holy Ghost, whom the Father will send in my name, he shall teach you all things, and bring all things to your remembrance, whatsoever I have said unto you. John 14:26 (KJV)

But the Comforter, which is the Holy Ghost, whom the Father will send in my name, he shall teach you all things, and bring all things to your remembrance, whatsoever I have said unto you. John 14:26 (KJV)

Early in the morning I will seek him

But the Comforter, which is the Holy Ghost, whom the Father will send in my name, he shall teach you all things, and bring all things to your remembrance, whatsoever I have said unto you. John 14:26 (KJV)

Date and Time of Dream: _____

_____

_____

_____

_____

_____

_____

_____

_____

_____

_____

_____

_____

_____

_____

_____

_____

_____

_____

_____

_____

_____

_____

But the Comforter, which is the Holy Ghost, whom the Father will send in my name, he shall teach you all things, and bring all things to your remembrance, whatsoever I have said unto you. John 14:26 (KJV)

But the Comforter, which is the Holy Ghost, whom the Father will send in my name, he shall teach you all things, and bring all things to your remembrance, whatsoever I have said unto you. John 14:26 (KJV)

But the Comforter, which is the Holy Ghost, whom the Father will send in my name, he shall teach you all things, and bring all things to your remembrance, whatsoever I have said unto you. John 14:26 (KJV)

But the Comforter, which is the Holy Ghost, whom the Father will send in my name, he shall teach you all things, and bring all things to your remembrance, whatsoever I have said unto you. John 14:26 (KJV)

Psalms 119:10 (KJV)

With my whole heart I have sought thee: O let me not wander from thy commandments

But the Comforter, which is the Holy Ghost, whom the Father will send in my name, he shall teach you all things, and bring all things to your remembrance, whatsoever I have said unto you. John 14:26 (KJV)

Date and Time of Dream: _____

_____

_____

_____

_____

_____

_____

_____

_____

_____

_____

_____

_____

_____

_____

_____

_____

_____

_____

But the Comforter, which is the Holy Ghost, whom the Father will send in my name, he shall teach you all things, and bring all things to your remembrance, whatsoever I have said unto you. John 14:26 (KJV)

But the Comforter, which is the Holy Ghost, whom the Father will send in my name, he shall teach you all things, and bring all things to your remembrance, whatsoever I have said unto you. John 14:26 (KJV)

But the Comforter, which is the Holy Ghost, whom the Father will send in my name, he shall teach you all things, and bring all things to your remembrance, whatsoever I have said unto you. John 14:26 (KJV)

But the Comforter, which is the Holy Ghost, whom the Father will send in my name, he shall teach you all things, and bring all things to your remembrance, whatsoever I have said unto you. John 14:26 (KJV)

Psalms 127:2 (KJV)
It is vain for you to rise up early,
to sit up late, to eat the bread of
sorrows; for so He giveth his
beloved sleep.

But the Comforter, which is the Holy Ghost, whom the Father will send in my name, he shall teach you all things, and bring all things to your remembrance, whatsoever I have said unto you. John 14:26 (KJV)

Date and Time of Dream: _____

_____

_____

_____

_____

_____

_____

_____

_____

_____

_____

_____

_____

_____

_____

_____

_____

_____

_____

But the Comforter, which is the Holy Ghost, whom the Father will send in my name, he shall teach you all things, and bring all things to your remembrance, whatsoever I have said unto you. John 14:26 (KJV)

But the Comforter, which is the Holy Ghost, whom the Father will send in my name, he shall teach you all things, and bring all things to your remembrance, whatsoever I have said unto you. John 14:26 (KJV)

But the Comforter, which is the Holy Ghost, whom the Father will send in my name, he shall teach you all things, and bring all things to your remembrance, whatsoever I have said unto you. John 14:26 (KJV)

But the Comforter, which is the Holy Ghost, whom the Father will send in my name, he shall teach you all things, and bring all things to your remembrance, whatsoever I have said unto you. John 14:26 (KJV)

Psalms 141:2 (NKJV)
Let my prayer be set before you as incense, the lifting up of my hands as the evening sacrifice.

But the Comforter, which is the Holy Ghost, whom the Father will send in my name, he shall teach you all things, and bring all things to your remembrance, whatsoever I have said unto you. John 14:26 (KJV)

Date and Time of Dream: _____

But the Comforter, which is the Holy Ghost, whom the Father will send in my name, he shall teach you all things, and bring all things to your remembrance, whatsoever I have said unto you. John 14:26 (KJV)

But the Comforter, which is the Holy Ghost, whom the Father will send in my name, he shall teach you all things, and bring all things to your remembrance, whatsoever I have said unto you. John 14:26 (KJV)

But the Comforter, which is the Holy Ghost, whom the Father will send in my name, he shall teach you all things, and bring all things to your remembrance, whatsoever I have said unto you. John 14:26 (KJV)

But the Comforter, which is the Holy Ghost, whom the Father will send in my name, he shall teach you all things, and bring all things to your remembrance, whatsoever I have said unto you. John 14:26 (KJV)

Psalms 63: 6-7 (KJV)

ଓଷ

6 When I remember you on my bed, I meditate on you in the night watches. 7 Because You have been my help, therefore in the shadow of Your wings I will rejoice.

ଓଷ

But the Comforter, which is the Holy Ghost, whom the Father will send in my name, he shall teach you all things, and bring all things to your remembrance, whatsoever I have said unto you. John 14:26 (KJV)

Date and Time of Dream: _____

But the Comforter, which is the Holy Ghost, whom the Father will send in my name, he shall teach you all things, and bring all things to your remembrance, whatsoever I have said unto you. John 14:26 (KJV)

But the Comforter, which is the Holy Ghost, whom the Father will send in my name, he shall teach you all things, and bring all things to your remembrance, whatsoever I have said unto you. John 14:26 (KJV)

But the Comforter, which is the Holy Ghost, whom the Father will send in my name, he shall teach you all things, and bring all things to your remembrance, whatsoever I have said unto you. John 14:26 (KJV)

But the Comforter, which is the Holy Ghost, whom the Father will send in my name, he shall teach you all things, and bring all things to your remembrance, whatsoever I have said unto you. John 14:26 (KJV)

Proverbs 3:24 (KJV)

24 When thou liest down, thou shalt not be afraid: yea, thou shalt lie down, and thy sleep shall be sweet.

But the Comforter, which is the Holy Ghost, whom the Father will send in my name, he shall teach you all things, and bring all things to your remembrance, whatsoever I have said unto you. John 14:26 (KJV)

Date and Time of Dream: _____

_____

_____

_____

_____

_____

_____

_____

_____

_____

_____

_____

_____

_____

_____

_____

_____

_____

But the Comforter, which is the Holy Ghost, whom the Father will send in my name, he shall teach you all things, and bring all things to your remembrance, whatsoever I have said unto you. John 14:26 (KJV)

But the Comforter, which is the Holy Ghost, whom the Father will send in my name, he shall teach you all things, and bring all things to your remembrance, whatsoever I have said unto you. John 14:26 (KJV)

But the Comforter, which is the Holy Ghost, whom the Father will send in my name, he shall teach you all things, and bring all things to your remembrance, whatsoever I have said unto you. John 14:26 (KJV)

But the Comforter, which is the Holy Ghost, whom the Father will send in my name, he shall teach you all things, and bring all things to your remembrance, whatsoever I have said unto you. John 14:26 (KJV)

Proverbs 8:17 King James Version (KJV)

17 I love them that love me; and those that seek me early shall find me.

But the Comforter, which is the Holy Ghost, whom the Father will send in my name, he shall teach you all things, and bring all things to your remembrance, whatsoever I have said unto you. John 14:26 (KJV)

Date and Time of Dream: _____

_____

_____

_____

_____

_____

_____

_____

_____

_____

_____

_____

_____

_____

_____

_____

_____

_____

But the Comforter, which is the Holy Ghost, whom the Father will send in my name, he shall teach you all things, and bring all things to your remembrance, whatsoever I have said unto you. John 14:26 (KJV)

But the Comforter, which is the Holy Ghost, whom the Father will send in my name, he shall teach you all things, and bring all things to your remembrance, whatsoever I have said unto you. John 14:26 (KJV)

But the Comforter, which is the Holy Ghost, whom the Father will send in my name, he shall teach you all things, and bring all things to your remembrance, whatsoever I have said unto you. John 14:26 (KJV)

But the Comforter, which is the Holy Ghost, whom the Father will send in my name, he shall teach you all things, and bring all things to your remembrance, whatsoever I have said unto you. John 14:26 (KJV)

Printed in Poland
by Amazon Fulfillment
Poland Sp. z o.o., Wrocław

54808976R00080